Extreme Animals

The Toughest Creatures on Earth

Nicola Davies

illustrated by **Neal Layton**

CANDLEWICK PRESS

6

THIS CANDLEWICK BOOK BELONGS TO:

me

your momma

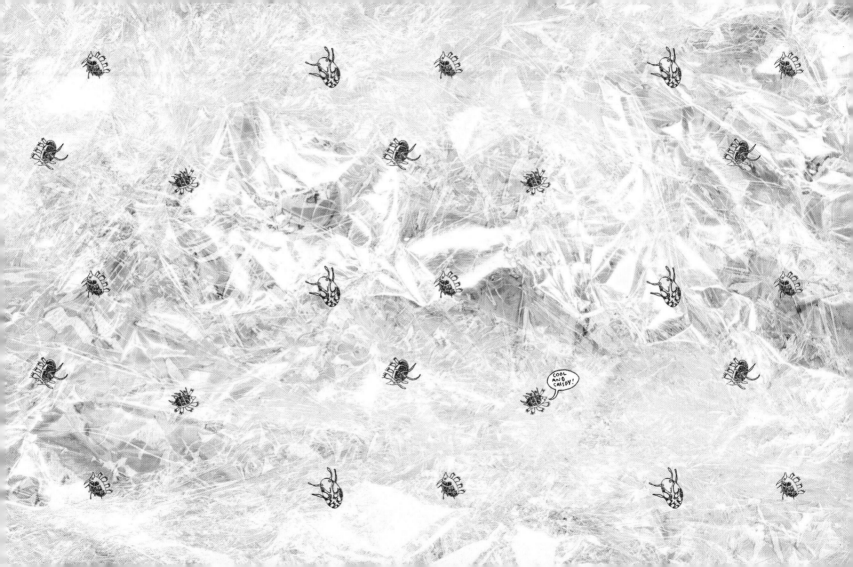

For Mike Shooter, with love — N. D.

For Alison — I'd be frozen, boiled, and squashed without you — N. L.

Text copyright © 2006 by Nicola Davies
Illustrations copyright © 2006 by Neal Layton

First U.S. paperback edition 2009

The Library of Congress has cataloged the hardcover edition as follows:

Davies, Nicola, date.
Extreme animals : the toughest creatures on earth /
by Nicola Davies ; illustrated by Neal Layton. — 1st U.S. ed.
p.   cm.
ISBN 978-0-7636-3067-6 (hardcover)
1. Animals — Adaptation — Juvenile literature. 2. Extreme environments —
Juvenile literature.   I. Layton, Neal, ill. II. Title.
QL49.D362 2006
590 — dc22   2005043544

ISBN 978-0-7636-4127-6 (paperback)

CCP 15 14 13
10 9 8 7 6 5 4

Printed in Shenzhen, Guangdong, China

This book was typeset in AT Arta.
The illustrations were done in ink and digitally colored.

Candlewick Press
99 Dover Street
Somerville, Massachusetts 02144

visit us at www.candlewick.com

THE TINY BACTERIA ON THE OPPOSITE PAGE ARE ENJOYING BEING BOILED ALIVE IN SUPER HOT MUD. YOU CAN FIND OUT WHY IF YOU TURN TO PAGE 37...

We humans are such a bunch of wimps!

We can't stand the cold,

we can't stand the heat,

we can't live without food, or water,

and just a few minutes without air is enough to finish us off.

Luckily, not all life is so fragile. All over the planet there are animals (and plants) that relish the sort of conditions that would kill a human quicker than you could say "coffin."

Keeping Out the Freeze

Let's start at the top — the top of our world: the Arctic region, where the North Pole is.

Up there, it's so cold in winter that the entire Arctic Ocean freezes over with ice that is yards thick. The inside of a freezer is around 0°F, but the Arctic can be much colder: down to -75°F. A bracing -20°F is about normal for an Arctic winter's day; at that temperature your bare flesh would freeze solid in sixty seconds.

To have any chance at all of survival, you'd need to wear:

THE TOP OF OUR WORLD

a hat

an extra hat

a down jacket and a fleece sweater

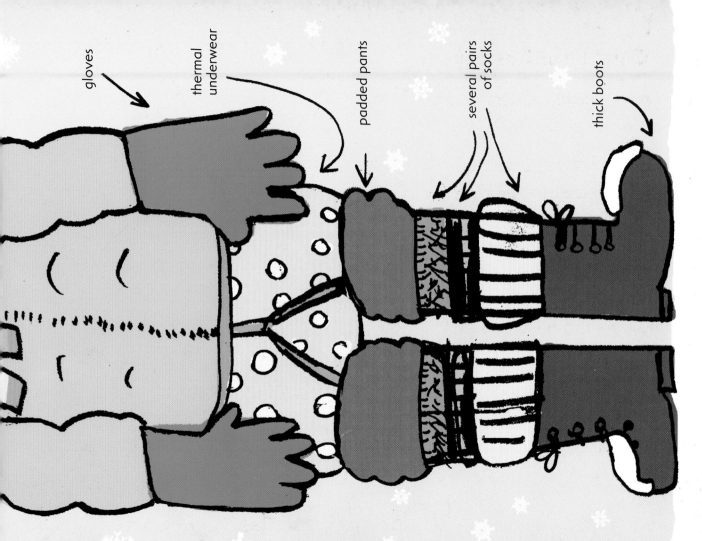

gloves

thermal underwear

padded pants

several pairs of socks

thick boots

Without all these warm layers, you'd be dead in minutes!
With them, you might just last a few days.

9

Yet polar bears stay constantly cozy . . . in the nude! That's because their birthday suits work better than our clothes. Instead of thermal underwear, polar bears have a three-inch layer of fat under their skin. Over that, they have a double layer of fur, which has an extra trick for beating cold: each hair is hollow and traps warm air like a mini quilt. Polar bear skin is special too: it's black! Dark colors absorb more heat than light colors — just take a walk in a black T-shirt on a hot day if you don't believe it — so any warmth that the fur traps soaks right into the bear's body.

ANOTHER LAYER OF FUR

LAYER OF FUR

3 inches

FAT

POLAR BEAR FAT/FUR DIAGRAM

LIVE NAKED

This all works so well that it fooled some scientists, who had decided that the best way to count bears was to scan the snow, from a plane, with heat-sensitive cameras. The snag was that polar bear body heat is so locked in that the outside of the fur is the same temperature as the snow. So the only thing that showed up was the occasional polar bear nose — since they're not covered in fur!

keep ~~cool~~ WARM

World's Coziest Coat

Polar bear fur could be the warmest on Earth, but there are other contenders for the title of World's Coziest Coat.

Arctic musk oxen have the warmest woolly coats. Their wool grows right down to their ankles and is eight times warmer than sheep's wool. (It even has a special name: qiviut, pronounced *KEE-vee-ut.*)

Sea otters have the densest fur on Earth, with almost one million hairs per square inch. They spend all their lives in extremely cold water, and their fine fur keeps a layer of warm air trapped next to their skin all the time.

Bowhead whales live in the Arctic Ocean, where the water is almost freezing all year round. Of course, they don't have any fur at all, but they do have a layer of fat under the skin almost two feet thick. You could say that it's the thickest underwear in the world.

But the title for world's coziest coat probably would have to go to the emperor penguin's coat of feathers. Emperor penguins live at the other end of the planet: the Antarctic, home of the South Pole. The Antarctic is the coldest place on Earth, where winter temperatures are between -4 and -125 °F. And winter is when emperor penguins choose to breed!

THE WINNER!

← AN EMPEROR PENGUIN

12

There's nowhere to nest, and nothing to make a nest with, so a male emperor penguin takes the one egg that his mate has laid and balances it on his feet. Then he stands around in the snow and hundred-mile-an-hour freezing winds for sixty-five days, until the egg hatches.

THE BOTTOM OF OUR WORLD

This sounds impossible — not to mention miserable and boring — but emperor dads manage it because of their amazing coat of feathers. It's more than an inch thick, with stiff feathers to keep the wind out and fluffy feathers to keep the warmth in. The coat is so good at keeping heat in and cold out that there can be a temperature difference of 140°F between the inside and outside of the feathers.

A feathery fold of skin keeps the egg cozy. But daddy penguins' feet have no heat-saving cover. So, to keep their body heat from leaking out that way, they use a "counter-current mechanism." This is a fancy way of saying that warm blood headed to the feet instead passes most of its heat to the cold blood going back into the body *from* the feet. So the feet are kept just barely warmer than freezing, but very little precious body heat ends up escaping through the tootsies.

I SEE IT'S SNOWING AGAIN.

YEAH, 100-MILE-AN-HOUR WINDS TOO.

EMPEROR PENGUIN DIAGRAM

Cold Cuddling

Having a warm coat isn't the only way to cheat life-threatening cold; sharing body heat also works remarkably well. Emperor penguins do it, gathering together in a huddle to beat the Antarctic chill. Very, very slowly, hundreds of penguins shuffle along, changing position, so that everyone gets a turn in the warm center of the huddle.

For very small birds, even an ordinary frosty winter night can be life-threateningly cold. Tiny birds like wrens just can't keep warm, so up to thirty of them will roost together. Cuddled up, they can survive temperatures that otherwise would have frozen them to the branch by morning.

Many birds and other animals use huddling to keep warm, but Inca doves from the southwestern United States and Mexico are the only ones that do it in formation. They make themselves into a living pyramid to warm up after the deep chill of winter nights.

True Toughness

Polar bears can keep warm in conditions that would kill a human, but in one important way, a polar bear is just as much of a wimp as we are: if its body temperature drops by more than a few degrees, it can die. The Truly Tough Animals are the ones that can let their bodies get really cold right through and still survive.

Some of the most delicate creatures on Earth are in fact Truly Tough. Hummingbirds can let their body temperatures drop 35 to 55 °F below normal. Just compare that with humans: if our temperature drops by 4 °F, we get sick, and a drop of 18 °F is likely to kill us. Yet hummingbirds do it almost every night to save on food. Keeping their bodies warm would use up food, and hummingbirds can't fly around feeding on nectar in the dark!

Food-saving makes some bats Truly Tough too. Most insects disappear in winter, so the bats that eat them have to live off their own body fat until spring. Keeping warm and active would burn those fat stores too fast, so bats hibernate and let their bodies get really cold, to make their fat stores last. Red bats from Canada and the U.S. get the coldest and can stand a body temperature as low as 23 °F for a short time. But that's their limit — any colder and their bodies start to burn fat to warm up again.

TRULY TOUGH

BUT DELICATE TOO !!

Frog Popsicles

Mammals and birds are warm-blooded, so they can burn food to keep warm. But other animals — such as reptiles and amphibians — are cold-blooded: their body temperature goes up and down with the temperature outside. The only way they can survive freezing temperatures is by hiding somewhere warm or by turning into an icicle for the winter!

Down in the freezing leaf litter of the forests where red bats hibernate, you can find wood frogs, frozen solid and brittle as glass. These "frogsicles" aren't dead, and in the springtime they will just thaw out and hop off into the sunshine.

Usually, being frozen solid is very, very bad for living things. That's because bodies are mostly made of water. When water freezes to ice — at a little below 32 °F — it expands (gets bigger) and breaks whatever happens to be holding it. (This is why water pipes in houses sometimes burst in cold weather.) When bodies freeze, ice bursts blood vessels and wrecks organs, like hearts and lungs, by cracking open their cells. (Cells are the tiny, delicate building blocks from which all bodies are made.)

How, then, do "frogsicles" survive? They do it by making the ice grow *between* all the important bits of their bodies, *outside* those teeny cells, where it can't do much harm.

Antifreeze (OR, PUT SOME BEETLE BLOOD IN YOUR CAR)

If an animal can't keep warm or can't survive turning into ice, what does it do in extreme cold? It uses antifreeze. Some animal antifreezes work in just the same way as the antifreeze we put in our cars: they make water freeze at a much lower temperature, so even if it gets colder than freezing, there's no ice formation.

To make sure that only the water *between* their cells freezes, wood frogs use sugar as antifreeze! They fill the water in their cells with it, lowering the freezing point way below zero, so that ice can't form and damage their bodies. But some fish have antifreeze that works in an even cleverer way: it sticks to the ice crystals, so they can't grow! Ice fish from the Antarctic Ocean live in water that is colder than the freezing point of most fish blood. But ice fish, and other fish like them, don't freeze, because their bodies are full of this clever antifreeze.

Polar seas don't ever get colder than a few degrees below freezing, but on land, Arctic and Antarctic temperatures can go down to -20, -70, or even -110°F. Resisting freezing in those conditions takes a very strong antifreeze indeed. And that is just what scientists have found in some polar insects. Some Arctic beetles and tiny Antarctic bugs called springtails, less than a tenth of an inch long, stay unfrozen in extreme polar cold because their ice-eating antifreeze is thirty times stronger than the one in fish! (Scientists get very excited about animal antifreezes because they hope to be able to copy them, to help us humans preserve food and to keep organs for transplant alive for much longer.)

ASTOUNDING!

Blowing Hot and Cold

Snowy poles and mountaintops aren't the only places where it gets horribly cold. Deserts, which are hot and dry during the day, can freeze at night because there are no clouds to keep the warmth in after the sun goes down. This gives desert animals a bit of a problem: it may be too hot by day for a thick coat of fur or feathers, so what do you do about the nighttime chill?

Roadrunners, long-legged birds from the deserts of the southern United States, have a special way of warming themselves up as soon as the sun rises, so they don't mind shivering throught the night. They turn their backs on the morning sun and lift their feathers so the nice warm rays shine onto a special strip of black skin across their shoulders. This skin soaks up the heat and warms each bird right through, like a heated shawl! In no time at all, they're as warm as toast and running about the desert at top speed.

The Camel Yo-yo

Roadrunners need the heat of the desert day to survive the cold desert nights. Camels are the other way around—they need the cold of the night to recover from the heat of the day, when temperatures can reach 110 or 120°F. We humans get sick if our temperatures go up more than a couple of degrees, and a rise of 11°F can be lethal. But camels let their temperatures go up and down like yo-yos, changing by as much as 14°F. At sunrise, after a chilly night, camels' bodies are quite cool. They get warmer and warmer all day, but by the time they're getting a bit too hot, the sun goes down and night cools them off again.

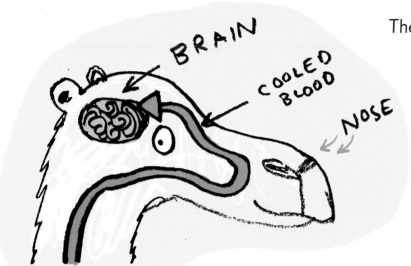

BRAIN

COOLED BLOOD

NOSE

The one part of a camel that can't cope with the daytime temperature rise of 14 °F is its brain. If it gets as hot as the rest of the camel, the brain will start to die. So blood on its way to the camel's brain is cooled by passing through blood vessels in the camel's long nose, where the air moving in and out carries away the heat. Only after the blood has been cooled does make it to the camel's brain.

That isn't quite the whole story, as a camel's fur has a part to play too. Instead of keeping heat in, the camel's fur keeps the heat out. Shaved camels get a lot hotter than furry ones! You'll find, if you ever go to a hot desert, that the best way to keep cool is by wearing quite a lot of clothes — especially a hat!

CHILL OUT, MAN!

THE DESERT DURING THE DAY

ZZZZZ...

ZZZZZ

HUNGRY MAMMALS

THE DESERT AT NIGHT

How to Live in a Desert

Letting your body temperature go up and down is a good way to cope with desert life. But most mammals can't do it. Our bodies just don't work properly unless we stay at a pretty even temperature. So desert mammals — apart from camels, of course — tend to stay hidden underground, where it's cooler, by day. They come out at night, when their ability to burn food and keep their bodies warm is useful.

Reptiles don't mind yo-yoing body temperatures; they're used to it. They can't make their own body heat, so they rely on the sun to warm them up and the shade to cool them down. They can't move around quickly when their bodies are chilled, though, so mostly they spend nights underground (out of the way of hungry mammals). They come out when there's sunshine to warm them. Many are quite comfortable if their body temperature goes up to over 100°F. Desert iguanas from the U.S. are happy up to 115°F, but if they start getting hotter than that, they have to lie down in the shade!

In the Sahara Desert in Africa, just as the reptiles run for cover, the ants come out. Silver ants can cope with a body temperature of 128°F, a few degrees more than the fringe-fingered lizards that like to eat them. So the ants can search for food without being eaten and claim the title of Hottest Animal in the Desert.

Dying for a Drink

Heat isn't the biggest problem in deserts: lack of water is. In 113 °F desert heat, you would need to sweat almost a gallon EVERY HOUR to keep your body from overheating. When camels have plenty of water to drink, they don't bother with all that body heat yo-yo stuff: they just sweat and keep cool.

But of course the main feature of deserts is NO water (which is why camels in the desert *don't* just sweat to keep cool. By the way, a camel's hump isn't full of water; it's fat, a store of food). And without water to replace all you'd lose in sweat, you'd dry out like a prune, then overheat too and be dead in about a day.

Most mammals — including humans — can't tolerate losing much more than a tenth of their bodies' water. What with that and not being able to put up with body temperatures of more than a few degrees above normal (unless they're camels, of course), mammals are doubly bad at desert living. But reptiles, as we've seen already, don't mind getting hot and so don't need to sweat to keep cool. They're also very resistant to drying out. For a start, they have thick, scaly skins that keep water safely inside their bodies. On top of that, they have special pee that uses up very little water. And, as a final aid to surviving heat and drought, desert reptiles can put up with losing most of their bodies' water, so they can survive for many months without drinking at all!

Fried, Dried, and Starved!

Reptiles are suited to desert life in another way, too: they're good at going without food! Mammals use energy from food to keep their bodies from getting too cold or too hot, so they need ten times more food than reptiles to keep them alive. And as food can be in short supply in a desert, being able to put up with starvation is very useful.

Insects and spiders are cold-blooded too, and even better at starving than reptiles, as a British naturalist, John Blackwell, found out more than 170 years ago. He put a spider in a jar on October 15, 1829, and it lived without food or water until April 30, 1831, more than eighteen months later! That's just the sort of survival skill you need for hanging around in webs in the corner of a room, hoping that a fly might pass!

Humans, like most mammals, as well as birds, are terrible at starving. The longest an average-size adult human could expect to last without food would be around forty days. But not all warm-blooded animals are so bad at it. Emperor penguins don't eat at all while they are incubating, nor on the long journey back to the sea after their eggs hatch. That's a total of 115 days without food! Polar bears do even better and can endure up to eight months without food. They use up all their fat reserves and even some of their muscles, so they are almost eating themselves alive!

Burning up your own body as food allows animals to survive times when food is scarce, but it's useful in other ways too: it can help with long-distance travel. Tiny blackpoll warblers migrate from North America to South America in an eighty-hour, nonstop flight. It's the energy equivalent of a human running 1,200 four-minute miles! The warblers do it by using their own bodies as fuel, so by the time they arrive, they are not much more than bone and feather, having lost half their body weight!

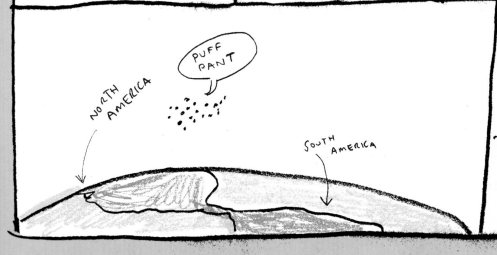

Into the Inferno

Polar wastes, desiccated deserts, and the insides of old glass jars! Is there anywhere on Earth that animals can't live? What about volcanoes? Molten magma, boiling pools of mud, and spouts of scalding water, all clouded in deadly gases — you'd think *nothing* could survive in such places — but you'd be wrong. If you could get close enough to look, without being burned to death, you'd see smears of color in the mud and water: red, orange, cloudy gray, and blue. These are colonies of bacteria, tiny living beings whose whole bodies are just one cell.

Bacteria live everywhere, but the bacteria that live near volcanoes are special. They are called thermophiles (which means "heat lovers") and they can *only* live where it's extremely hot — between 176 and 230°F. Thermophiles don't only love being boiled: many also enjoy conditions that would suffocate or poison a human being. Most eat chemicals like sulfur and iron for energy, and nearly all would be killed by ordinary oxygen. Nobody knows exactly *how* these tiny single-celled beings survive, but scientists do know *why* they live this way. Billions of years ago, when thermophiles evolved, Earth was covered in volcanoes and boiling seas of sulfuric acid: there wasn't even any air, just poisonous gas. As far as thermophiles are concerned, things haven't changed a bit!

CLOSE-UP OF THERMOPHILE BACTERIA

IRON

SULFUR

Yum!

Black Smokers

Thermophiles live wherever the hot, melted heart of the Earth bubbles up, even at the very bottom of the sea. Down there, you can find plumes of super-hot water streaming up from the molten rock below. These are called black smokers, and thermophiles live here by the millions, bathing in the boiling water and eating chemicals. They aren't alone, either. Where cold seawater

MORE THERMOPHILES

cools the super-heated plumes, eyeless shrimp, giant worms, and other weird creatures eat the thermophiles, and each other! It's a whole other world that doesn't need sunlight and would go on existing even if our sun went out. Black smokers could even give us some clues about how life might exist on other planets.

The Squash Factor

In fact, scientists actually know more about the surface of the moon than they know about the very bottom of our own oceans. One reason for that is pressure — the squash factor. The deeper you go under the ocean, the greater the weight of water pressing down on you. For every 33 feet you go down, the pressure increases by one "atmosphere" — the weight of the air at sea level. So if you dived to the deepest place in the ocean, the bottom of the Mariana Trench, 6.8 miles below the surface, there would be 1,100 atmospheres pressing down on you. All the air-filled bits of your body, like your lungs, would be squashed flat, and you'd be unable to breathe. You'd also suffer from High Pressure Nervous Syndrome (HPNS), which would make you shake uncontrollably and pass out a lot.

Instead, you would need to go down in something that looks more like a spacecraft from a science-fiction movie: a submersible, with a very thick hull to resist that super-squashing pressure and big headlights to see with, because the deep sea is completely dark. All sorts of weird and wonderful animals would loom in the headlights: hatchetfish, gulper eels, tripod fish, luminous squid, and starfish on stalks. And not one of them would seem bothered by that huge weight of water. They certainly wouldn't look squashed. That's because they don't have air-filled body parts, like lungs, to squash! What's more, their nervous systems are adapted for life at depth; *they* get the symptoms of HPNS in *shallow* water!

Bubbles in the Blood

You probably don't need to be reminded that humans have to breathe air, so if we want to stay under water for longer than a couple of minutes, we have to take our air supply with us. And that air supply has to be under the same pressure as the pressure of water squashing our rib cages — or it wouldn't stand a chance of getting into our lungs. Under high pressure like that, air can dissolve in the blood. As soon as a deep-sea diver comes back to the surface and the pressure is off, that air reforms as bubbles. Think of a soda bottle with the lid firmly on and the drink inside under pressure: take off the lid, and there's an immediate fizz of bubbles. Now imagine that happening to the human body. Ouch! It's very painful and potentially fatal. It's called the bends, and human divers have to come to the surface very slowly to avoid it.

Yet sperm whales dive to depths of more than 3,200 feet, and elephant seals go down to 5,150 feet, all without a touch of the bends! How? Both whales and seals breathe out when they dive, then, at around 160 feet below the surface, their ribs fold flat and their lungs are squashed empty. So there's no air in the lungs to be forced into their blood. This way they can stay down for thirty to fifty minutes and pop back up without the ghost of a fizz. (And how do they manage without breathing for so long? By storing oxygen in their blood and muscles before they dive!)

Feel the Force of "g"

SPLAT!!

If you do decide that exploring space seems less risky than exploring the deep ocean, you will have to deal with another kind of squash factor. You've probably experienced it already if you've been on a fast amusement park ride — the ride spins faster and faster and you are pressed into your seat, as if someone were sitting on your chest! This is the effect of the "g-force." Gravity is the force that stops you from falling off the Earth and makes buttered toast drop on the floor. Gravity is measured in *gs*. Just standing still, a force of 1 *g* is what keeps your feet on the ground. If you start to accelerate, in an amusement park ride for instance, or even worse a jet aircraft, the g-force grows. It pins you into your seat and pulls all your blood to your feet. At around 5 *g*, the blood just can't make it to your brain anymore, and you pass out. Fighter pilots in World War II experienced huge g-forces when flying fast turns, and regularly blacked out. Nowadays, jet pilots wear special G suits, which squeeze the blood up from their legs to their heads to keep that from happening. All the same, U.S. Air Force recruits must pass a test that shows they can stay conscious at 7.5 *g* for sixteen seconds. The maximum g-force the human skeleton can stand is 25 *g* — any more than that, and our bones start to break!

USAF

¡¡ OOH OOM

GERONIMO!

INSECT WORLD

In the insect world, 25 g is nothing. A flea can jump 130 times its own height, somersaulting at high speed as it does, and experiencing a force of 200 g. Click beetles can jump even faster and survive 400 g. As the click beetle spins in the air, its head suffers up to 2,000 g, yet click beetles never seem to pass out! (The scientist who measured this says that click beetle brains aren't damaged, as ours would be, because click beetles aren't very bright anyway!)

Sponge Smoothie and the History of Life

Whales and click beetles suffer huge squashing forces and still stay in one piece. They are really just squash resistors. To be a Truly Tough Animal, you have to be a squash *survivor*, and stay alive even if your body is in bits! Quite a lot of invertebrates (that's animals without bones, like insects, worms, crabs, and snails) are good at this, because their bodies are simple and easier to make than big, complicated animals like us. Worms can be chopped in two and grow a new other half. Starfish can be cut to bits and each bit will become a new starfish (something that divers in Australia found out rather too late, when they tried to get rid of a plague of crown-of-thorns starfish on the Great Barrier Reef by chopping them up).

Sponges are the toughest of all. They live in the sea and come in all shapes and sizes, from tiny flat ones to huge chimney-shaped ones. You might even have used the dead, rubbery insides of one to wash yourself in the bath! To be honest, even live sponges don't do much: they just sort of sit there and grow. But put one in a blender and you'll see that they do something no other animal can: pour your sponge smoothie back into its seawater home, and it will put itself back together. All the tiny little bits of sponge will find each other and slowly rebuild the whole animal!

The reason that sponges can do this is an important part of the history of life on Earth.

Once Upon a Time...

all living things were tiny, each made of just one cell, like bacteria. Then some of these single-celled beings started living together in colonies and found that things were easier if some cells got food and the others did the cleaning (as it were). Over time, these colonies got bigger and more complicated, with more and more different jobs. At last, cells in these colonies couldn't survive on their own: they had become a multicellular organism, a being made of lots of different cells.

(Sponges are from an early part of this story. We have thousands of different kinds of cells in our bodies, but sponges have only about four. Their cells aren't completely helpless on their own, as one of our body cells would be, but they do like living together. So, when they get parted in the blender, they find their way back to each other, just as the first colonies of cells did millions of years ago.)

And they all lived happily ever after.

Except they didn't, because not even the Princess and the Handsome Prince live EVER after. Living things can resist cold, heat, pressure, starvation, poisoning, and suffocation, but they can't resist time. In the end, time gets us all.

TICK!
TICK!
TICK!

A YEW TREE

GIANT ALDABRAN TORTOISE

A TEACHER

A BRISTLE CONE PINE TREE THAT LIVES IN NEVADA

Holding Back Time

Living bodies are designed to last only long enough to reproduce and see their offspring safely into the world. Humans, along with elephants, take ages having babies and bringing them up, so we do pretty well in the Time Resistance stakes. We can all expect to live seventy or eighty years — with luck, perhaps a little longer. That's very good compared with "live fast, die young" mice, who are lucky to see their second birthdays, but it's nothing like a world record. The longest-lived animal is the very slow-maturing giant Aldabran tortoise. A male of this species was given as a present to the French army on the island of Mauritius in the Indian Ocean in 1766. It lived until 1918, when it fell down a gun

emplacement and was killed. Shall I do the math, or will you? Oh, OK. That means it was 152 years old—probably even older, as it was fully grown when it arrived on Mauritius.

Compared with the longest-lived plants, however, tortoises are only babies. Yew trees, the big, somber trees seen in British churchyards, can live for more than one thousand years, but the oldest trees live in California and Nevada. They are bristlecone pines, and scientists think they could have been growing for five thousand years—which would make them *even* older than most teachers!

Time Travelers

Studying how living things survive in volcanoes or in the sunless depths of the sea gives us a glimpse of what life might be like on other planets; studying how plants and animals survive time might help us to travel to those planets.

Space is vast. Even light, the fastest thing in the universe, takes four years and three months to get here from our nearest star, Alpha Centauri (actually three stars together). Spacecraft travel a lot more slowly than light. It took *Mars Express* nearly seven months to get to Mars, which is just over three minutes away at light speed. So it would take a spacecraft many, many years to travel to Alpha Centauri. If we want to go even farther, it's going to take several human lifetimes of reading in-flight magazines.

We need to be able to do what some seeds can do — go into a state in which life is kept on hold. Some seeds can lie dormant for hundreds, or even thousands, of years. A seed of the sacred lotus plant sprouted and grew after lying in a lake in China for more than 1,200 years. Seeds of sorghum, a tropical crop plant, can survive six thousand years of waiting and still spring to life.

How do they do it? Scientists are still trying to find out, so it'll be quite a while before humans are "boldly going" anywhere far in the real universe.

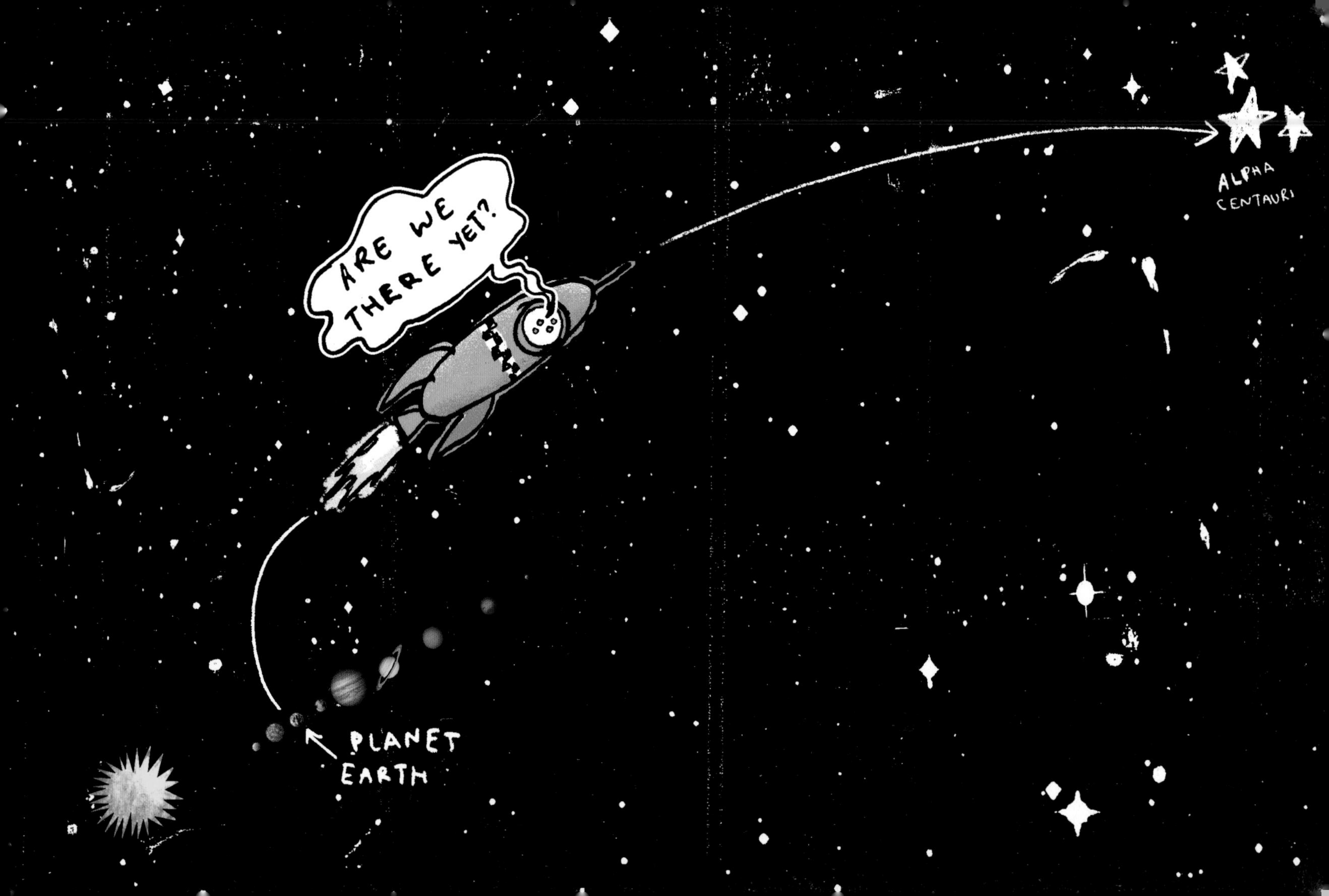
ARE WE THERE YET?
ALPHA CENTAURI
PLANET EARTH

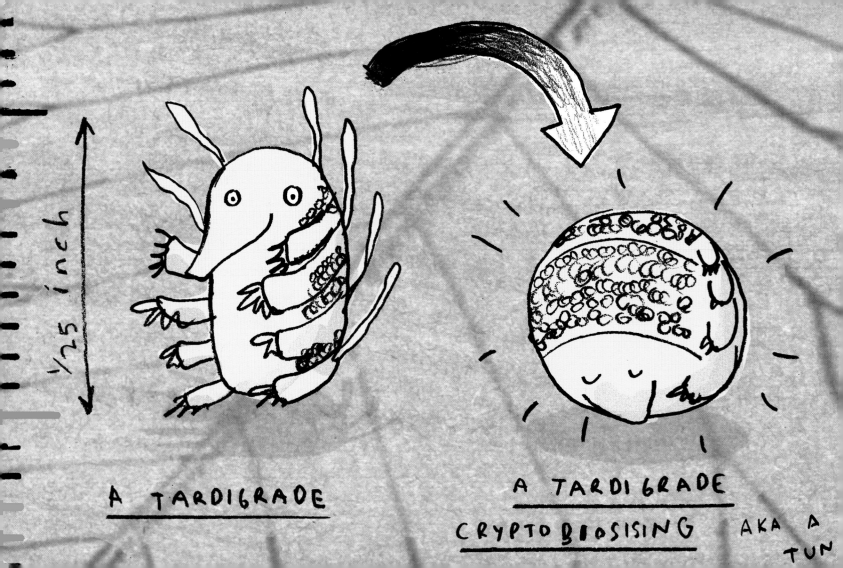

1/25 inch

A TARDIGRADE

A TARDIGRADE CRYPTOBIOSISING AKA A TUN

The Toughest Creature on Earth

In this book we've been all over the planet, to deserts, poles, volcanoes, and even to the bottom of the sea, to find living things that are much, much tougher than human beings. But if you want to find the Truly Toughest Extreme Animal, the all-around champion, that can survive being frozen, boiled, squashed, and quite a few other trials besides, you probably don't need to go farther than your local park or garden.

This celebrity creature lives quietly in films of water on plant leaves. (You could also find it in ponds or in the sea.) It isn't big or spectacular—the largest is just over 1/25 of an inch long. Its tiny, rounded body is divided into segments, and it has four pairs of little fat legs. It is a water bear, or tardigrade. Tardigrades don't have big eyes or fluffy fur, but there is something rather cute about them. They are mysterious little creatures, belonging to a very ancient group of animals that appeared on Earth more than 530 million years ago!

During their long history on Earth, tardigrades have evolved to survive anything by entering a state scientists call cryptobiosis (which means "hidden life"). At the first sign of trouble—a spot of drought or a cold snap—tardigrades pull in their limbs and fold up their whole bodies, like a telescope. They fill their cells with sugar to preserve them, like the sugar in jam, and they dry out, losing all but one percent of their bodies' water. In this state, which is called a tun, they seem indestructible.

Scientists have heated tuns to 300 °F — that's about one and a half times the boiling point. They've frozen them to absolute zero, the lowest possible temperature in the universe, -459 °F. They've put them under six times the pressure you'd find at the bottom of the ocean, and under no pressure at all, like the vacuum of outer space. They've zapped them with X-rays a thousand times stronger than a lethal dose for humans, and they've poisoned them with chemicals. The result is always the same: when the danger is past and the tun is returned to its home in the water, its limbs pop out, its body unfolds, and it goes about its business as if nothing at all had happened. There is even evidence to suggest that tuns could survive in their cryptobiotic state for hundreds, or even thousands, of years, making tardigrades almost immortal.

Tardigrade tuns are so tiny and light that they can blow around the planet in the wind. Perhaps they could travel high into the atmosphere and possibly even farther! Could it be that the first Earthling to colonize another world in space will be a tardigrade?

They're certainly tough enough!

INDEX

A

Alpha Centauri 54
amphibians 20
Antarctic 12–16, 23
Antarctic Ocean 23
Antarctic springtails 23
antifreezes 23
Arctic 8–9, 23
Arctic beetles 23
Arctic musk oxen 12–13
Arctic Ocean 8, 12
atmospheres 40

B

bacteria 37–39, 50
bats 19
bends, the 42
black smokers 38–39
Blackpoll warblers 34–35
bowhead whales 12–13
bristlecone pine tree 52–53

C

camels 26–27
cells 20, 50–51
click beetles 46–47, 49
coats 12–13
cold-blooded 20, 33
counter-current mechanism 15
crown-of-thorns starfish 49
cryptobiosis 56–58

D

desert iguanas 29
deserts 24–31, 33
divers 42, 49

E

elephant seals 42
elephants 52–53
Emperor penguins 12–17, 34

F

fleas 46
food 19, 20, 33
fringe-fingered lizards 29

G

g-force 44–45
giant Aldabran tortoise 52–53
gravity 45
gulper eels 41

H

hatchetfish 41
hibernation 19, 20
High Pressure Nervous
    Syndrome (HPNS) 40–41
humans 7–9, 23, 26, 30, 34,
    40, 42, 45, 52, 54–55
hummingbirds 19

I

ice fish 23
Inca doves 16

insects

insects 19, 23, 32–33,
    46–47, 49
invertebrates 49

L

light, speed of 54
luminous squid 41

M

mammals 29, 30, 34
Mariana Trench 40
Mars 54
Mars Express 54
mice 52–53

N

North Pole 8–9

O

oceans 38–43

P

polar bears 10–11, 19, 34
pressure 40–41, 45

IT'S ME AGAIN!!

Q
qiviut 12–13

R
red bats 19
reptiles 29, 30–31, 33
roadrunners 24–26

S
sacred lotus plant 54
Sahara Desert 29
sea otters 12–13
seeds 54
shrimp 39
silver ants 29
snails 49
sorghum plant 54
South Pole 12
sperm whales 42–43, 49
spiders 32–33
sponges 48–51

starfish 41, 48–49
starvation 33–34
sweat 30–31

T
tardigrades 56–59
thermophiles 37–39
time 52–55
tripod fish 41
tuns 57–59

V
volcanoes 36–39

W
warm-blooded 20
water 30
wood frogs 20–21, 23
worms 39, 48–49
wrens 16

Y
yew trees 52–53

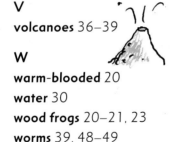

GLOSSARY

Antarctic the cold, frozen region around the South Pole, where penguins live

Arctic the cold, frozen region around the North Pole, where polar bears live

bacteria tiny living things whose bodies are just one simple cell

black smokers cracks in the sea bed where super-hot mineral-rich water streams up like smoke

cells tiny units, too small to see, from which all living bodies are made

cold-blooded not being able to keep warm when it's cold or cool when it's hot. The body temperatures of reptiles, amphibians, and fish go up and down with the temperature of their environment.

dormancy a sleeplike state. Dormant seeds and plants are alive but not growing, and can survive like that for years.

hibernation how some animals survive the winter: they go into a deep sleep for weeks or even months, using up their body fat instead of eating.

incubation keeping eggs warm so a baby can grow inside

magma red-hot melted rock that fills the center of the Earth like the filling in a chocolate

organs groups of different sorts of cells working together to do a job. The brain, heart, lungs, liver, skin, and kidneys are all organs.

warm-blooded being able to keep warm when it's cold and cool when it's hot. Birds and mammals are warm-blooded.

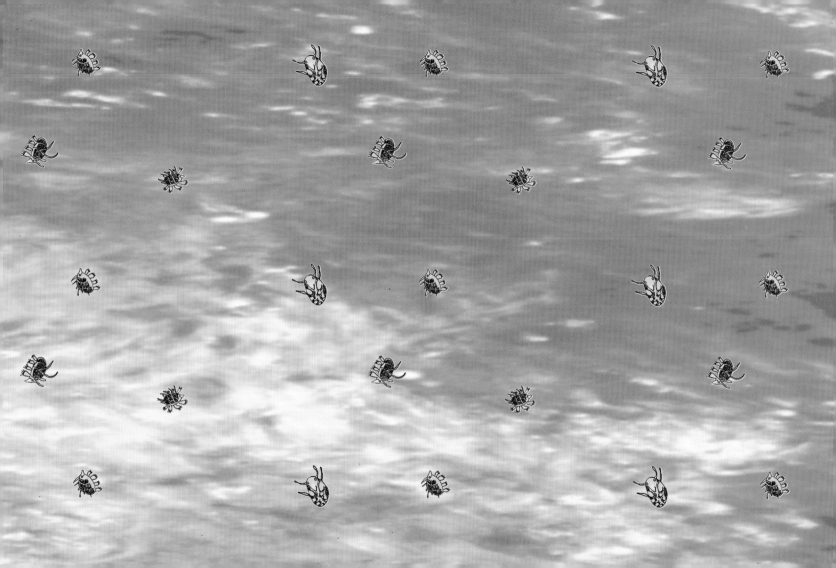

Nicola Davies earned a degree in zoology before becoming a writer, producer, and presenter of radio and television programs. Her many acclaimed nonfiction books for children include *Poop: A Natural History of the Unmentionable* and *What's Eating You? Parasites—The Inside Story*. She says, "I went to the Arctic a few years ago, and I froze! I had lots of high-tech clothing, and I was still cold all the time. Yet the Arctic animals that I saw had nothing but their own bodies to keep out the cold, and they seemed perfectly happy in the ice and snow. I was impressed, and the idea for this book was born."

Neal Layton received distinction for his MA in illustration from Central Saint Martins College of Art and Design, in London, and has been illustrating books for children ever since. He says, "Working on *Extreme Animals* was not only a lot of fun, but I also learned loads. It was challenging trying to visualize some of the things the book deals with, like intense heat and cold, but it was most difficult trying to draw extreme pressure—since you can't see it!"